# MIRACLE ON COVID STREET

JESSICA HARRIS

Miracle On Covid Street

Cover design by Victorine Lieske.
Edited by Kameo Monson.

❋ Created with Vellum

# TABLE OF CONTENTS

*To Daddy, who put your life on hold for forty-four days, so that you could be with me in Savannah. Thank you for the love you've shown me my entire life, but especially throughout those tough days. Also to Mama, who became "mama" to my boys while I fought such a horrible virus. Both of you spent countless hours praying as well as being the hands and feet of Christ. I love you both more than you'll ever know!*

# 1

## INTRODUCTIONS

"THE POINT IS THIS: WHOEVER SOWS SPARINGLY WILL ALSO REAP SPARINGLY, AND WHOEVER SOWS BOUNTIFULLY WILL ALSO REAP BOUNTIFULLY" (2 CORINTHIANS 9:6).

*T*his is a true story of faith, the power of prayer, and my determination to live. I was raised in the Baptist church from the time I was born. My parents took me to church almost every time the doors were open. Daddy sang in a gospel quartet when I was young, and I gave my life to Christ one night on my way home from a sing. I was baptized at the age of twelve.

You get the picture.

After growing up, I did the usual things: I went to college and got married. Chris is my now-ex-husband. We were married during the time of my COVID battle. But I should back up a bit and introduce my family. Chris and I have three boys: Kaleb, Kameron, and Kason. Then there's my daddy, Bruce, and the rest of my family. Daddy is a retired school teacher. He is also our church's music director and serves on the local board of education. His wife's name is Karen, and they have been married for thirty-one years. Karen has one daughter, Karla. Karla is married to Benji, and they have three kids: Klaire, Kenly, and Trey. My mama's name is Debra. She works at a local hospital, which also happens to be where I am currently employed. Her husband's name is Fred, and they have been married for thirty-one years. I have one brother, Justin. His wife's name is Mallory. They have two children: Emmaline and Jaxon. Fred has a daughter named Rachel. Rachel's family consists of her husband, Jordan, and their two kids, Nathan and Brinley. My Papa is Jesse. He's my maternal grandfather and only living grandparent.

Now that you know who everyone is, let's dive into my life.

Throughout high school, I participated in every youth group activity that I could. I was on the Youth Leadership Team and poured myself into the church during my senior year. Music has always been a huge part of my life, mostly due to being raised by a daddy in a quartet and two parents who played the piano. As a part of my high school classes, I also took a couple of early childhood education classes, which allowed me to go to the local elementary school and work with the teachers and students. This is where my love of children seems to have begun.

Although I didn't complete my bachelor's degree, I did go to college for elementary education. My love of children and Jesus continued to blossom throughout college. The only reason I didn't finish my college degree is because I got married and started a family of my own, with our oldest son, Kaleb, being born almost a year after the wedding.

## SURROGACY

"BEHOLD, CHILDREN ARE A HERITAGE FROM THE LORD, THE
FRUIT OF THE WOMB A REWARD" (PSALM 127:3).

*F*ast forward a decade. On November 4, 2018, I saw a post from a friend asking about a gestational surrogate for a friend of hers. Surrogacy is something I had heard of before, but had never looked too much into it. I honestly didn't think anything would come from the post because I knew that my friend was from Texas and figured her other friend was too. I commented that I had been thinking about it for years, but had never looked into it. Her friend messaged me back, and we formed a fast friendship. I constantly prayed for several days, asking God about everything, and it seemed that all of the pieces were falling into place.

My husband, Chris, wasn't initially on board with the surrogacy because he didn't know the process. We talked at length and I explained precisely what surrogacy was and how it worked, and he became supportive.

I flew to Fort Worth within three weeks to see her fertility doctor. By mid-February, all of the leg-work was complete and I underwent in vitro fertilization to transfer the couple's embryo into my uterus. After a rocky start with low HCG levels, the pregnancy was smooth and everything went very well. They flew me to Texas in July for a baby shower and to meet some friends and family.

Chris was an over-the-road truck driver at that time and was typically gone from Sunday night to Friday night. Before this job, he worked locally and our marriage seemed to struggle some. We would argue a bit, but we also chalked that up to "that's how all marriages go" and went on about our business. While he was on the road, our marriage improved significantly, so in mid-September, when he told me that he was considering taking a driving position that would allow him to be home every night, I told him we needed to pray about this. Since the boys and I had been home the majority of the time by ourselves for four years, our schedule was about to be disrupted. Still, I was also concerned that our marriage would begin to have problems again. Little did I know that God was already preparing us for what was about to happen with the surrogate baby that I was carrying.

October 1, 2019, Chris started the new position, and we began the transition of having him home every night. Things were going better than I had expected as far as our marriage was concerned. Two weeks later, on October 15, 2019, I was sitting on the couch, watching television before bed, when I realized I had not felt the baby move in a while. That was one of the most challenging realizations a pregnant woman can encounter. I honestly could not remember when I'd felt him move last. I was terrified, nervous, anxious, and just about any other negative emotion you can imagine. My head was spinning and it felt as if my heart was being ripped out of my chest. What would I tell the baby's mama? She was in my hometown, awaiting his arrival. We went to the hospital, and I prepared Chris for what I knew would happen. They wouldn't let him in with me until they knew for sure what was happening. We found out around 10:30 that evening that the baby had passed away. He was born at 9:21 the following morning. My family, church family, and friends surrounded me in prayer from near and far. There were a few from my immediate family, as well as my pastor and associate pastor, with me at the hospital as the baby was delivered.

I knew immediately that God was telling me that I was not done with surrogacy. In November of the same year, I began talking to a family from the Atlanta area about a second journey. I spoke with their doctor to make sure that the loss of the first sweet baby would not in any way hinder or render the process impossible. I was beyond excited that he believed the chance of loss happening again was slim. After many prayers, the intended parents and I agreed that we were a good match for each other and that we should move forward. Chris and I were on the same page that surrogacy was something we wanted to pursue again.

It was during this time that I was diagnosed with an autoimmune disease called Graves' disease. This is something that causes an overactive thyroid. After taking several months to get it under control, I could finally begin the requirements to move forward with the pregnancy. No time was wasted. On January 28, 2021, the in vitro transfer was completed. Their sweet boy was due to be born on the first surrogate baby's second birthday. His due date seemed to be a confirmation to his mother and myself that God had His hand in the entire process.

During my pregnancy with Baby E (my name for the baby I was carrying during the second surrogacy), my prenatal care was transferred to the high-risk obstetricians in Savannah, due to my age, the previous pregnancy loss, and my elevated blood pressure.

COVID-19 was becoming a bigger and bigger issue in the world. But, I never worried about COVID and felt the pandemic was being used as an agenda. At the time, I didn't personally know anyone who had been seriously sick with the virus and I didn't believe it was as serious or virulent as it was portrayed.

Since I had already experienced full-term pregnancy loss and there weren't any studies done on the vaccine during pregnancy, my family, with consideration for the baby's parents, decided not to get vaccinated. I did not want to do anything that might increase my risk of pregnancy loss.

# 3

# COVID DIAGNOSIS

"CASTING ALL YOUR CARES ON HIM, FOR HE CARES FOR
YOU" (1 PETER 5:7).

*I* pulled my boys from public school in 2018 because we felt like that was the best thing for our family at the time. The boys had asked to return to public school for the 2020-2021 school year, but we decided to wait another year to see how things developed with COVID.

When August rolled around, my boys went to public school after being homeschooled for three years.

On August 15, 2021, my son Kason started coughing. I decided to take him to get a COVID test the following morning. My step-mom had tested positive the Wednesday prior. I felt like my daddy might have had it as well, even though he'd tested negative. While I was getting Kason tested, I had myself tested, just to be safe. I tested positive, and Kason tested negative. At this point, I wasn't too scared about having the virus. Since we were eighteen months into the pandemic, I knew of people who had contracted it and been ok. The ones that I knew who had passed away also had other major health concerns. Looking back, I know that I also had some of those health concerns, but that never crossed my mind until later.

I called Chris, and he came home from work and took our older boys to be tested. Kaleb also tested positive. By Wednesday, all five of us had tested positive.

The boys and Chris were given medicines to treat their symptoms, as well as Ivermectin and an antibiotic to try to ward off pneumonia. Not a single doctor would prescribe me anything, not even the antibiotics that the rest of my family received that were supposedly safe for pregnant women. That was extremely frustrating for me. While I understood that the doctors were trying to remain cautious, I knew from past pregnancies of my own that there were medications, such as the antibiotics that the rest of my family were given, available that were safe for me. Mama went to the pharmacy to at least get me cough syrup. But when the pharmacist realized that it was for me, knowing that I was pregnant with COVID, he would not sell it to her. Mama was frustrated, but she came home without it.

My time was primarily spent in bed. Mama would call and make me go outside and walk down the driveway so that she knew I was moving around at least a little bit, but after a day or two, it became difficult for me to do much moving around. I scheduled an appointment with my obstetrician to try to get medicine as well as make sure the baby was doing well, and I managed to drive myself the two hours to the office. By the time I arrived, I was feeling so sick that I threw up in the parking lot. I eventually made it to the third-floor office and had an ultrasound. Because of the positive diagnosis, I couldn't go through the office's main entrance. They took me through a back door and straight into a room that was disinfected and closed off to the rest of the office. They offered me an antibody infusion, but I didn't agree to it right away. I wanted to make sure that it was safe for the baby.

Over the next two weeks, I became progressively worse. The first week, I tried to get up and move around as best I could, but my entire body hurt and I was worn out before I could get from my room to the back door.

By the beginning of the second week, I could barely get out of bed, and I certainly was not able to eat or drink anything. I made a trip to the emergency room on August 23rd to get fluids and some nausea medicine. After a couple of days, Chris realized that the nausea medicine was not helping. It just knocked me out. This made staying active, eating, and drinking even harder.

On Thursday of week two, August 26th, I had an antibody infusion in Savannah. I ended up staying at a nurse's house in Screven that night so that she could keep an eye on me and try to make me walk and drink. She was trying to make me walk because being mobile seemed to help patients not get as sick as the ones who stayed in bed. I felt a little bit better the next day, and my daddy came and picked me up and rode me around in his side-by-side (ATV) to get some fresh air and sunshine. I spent the next night at his house. While watching television on Friday night, I started having contractions and ended up having to call an ambulance. The contractions were between three and four minutes apart, so we decided that the ambulance was the best choice based on my previous rapid labors (four hours or less) and the fact that I was only 33 weeks pregnant. We were worried due to how early in the pregnancy it was, but I knew there was a good chance that the labor could be stopped. Once at the hospital, I was given fluids and two doses of tocolytics— medicine to stop the labor. After the contractions settled down, I was released back to Daddy's house.

# 4

# HOSPITALIZATION AND TRANSFER TO MEMORIAL HEALTH

"FOR I KNOW THE PLANS I HAVE FOR YOU, DECLARES THE LORD, PLANS TO PROSPER YOU AND NOT TO HARM YOU, PLANS TO GIVE YOU HOPE AND A FUTURE" (JEREMIAH 29:11).

*D*uring the next few days, I was able to begin eating a little bit and was also able to walk around the house some. I decided to check my oxygen levels on Wednesday, September 1, 2021, and it was in the eighties (normal levels are between 97 and 100 percent for someone without an existing lung condition). The reading is called an oxygen saturation (this is where the term "sats" comes from) and it measures the percentage of oxygen-saturated hemoglobin compared to the total hemoglobin in the body. I called Chris, and he had Papa bring me his oxygen concentrator. I began using oxygen. I called my high-risk OB in Savannah to inform them about my low levels, and they wanted me to go to the emergency room. I was instructed not to travel to Savannah, due to the distance, but to go to Wayne Memorial Hospital in Jesup, Georgia instead.

Of course, because of COVID rules, no one could go in with me, so I was alone. During the entire COVID outbreak, it was known that visitors were not allowed inside hospitals. While I understood that they were trying to limit exposure to COVID, it was frightening to think about people being isolated from their friends and family during such a scary time. I was frustrated and scared to be there alone. Most of the time, I was very quiet and didn't know how to speak up for myself. Because I was hesitant to ask questions, my fears and insecurities were exacerbated.

I had a chest x-ray and called my mama and Chris to tell them I was being admitted to the hospital because my lungs were full of pneumonia. I was put on the medical floor and on a high-flow nasal cannula because the regular oxygen cannula was not pushing enough oxygen to my lungs to keep my saturations up. This meant a thicker tube running across my face. I believe I was up to fifteen liters of oxygen per minute while on the high-flow cannula. One of the doctors told us that I did not have pneumonia but had pneumonitis. This is an infection in the lung's lining and is not as severe. I had a lot of trouble keeping my oxygen up when I had to move around or get up to use the bathroom. I remember my level dropping into the seventies a few times, which scared me.

I was still not allowed to have visitors, but they did let Mama come up to see me a few times since she worked on the next floor down. Over Labor Day weekend, Mama was able to arrange special privileges, and they let Chris come and stay with me, but he was not allowed to leave my room at all. He was going to stay from Friday to Sunday. When it came time for him to leave, Sunday afternoon, my anxiety spiked and he decided to stay until Monday. I was making small improvements and, by Wednesday, was able to switch back to a regular nasal cannula on five liters of oxygen.

At this point, we were under the impression that I would likely be going home the next day. Plans quickly changed. Dr. Mager, who is my regular (non-high-risk) OBGYN, got word that I was in the hospital with COVID, and she insisted that I be moved to Memorial Health University Hospital in Savannah, Georgia. She coordinated with the OBs in Savannah, and they worked right away on getting me a room. The hospitalist, which is the doctor employed by the hospital to treat patients without a primary care physician, told Mama that if I were his wife, daughter, or mama, that he would want me in Savannah. I felt like it was an unnecessary trip; however, after a couple of conversations with Chris, Mama, Daddy, and a couple of the nurses, we decided to just go ahead and make the trip and let them monitor me and the baby.

Chris came to Jesup to see me off, and I cried as they closed the doors to the ambulance. The trip to Savannah was pretty uneventful. Many text messages were sent from my family and members of our church praise team. During the hour and a half trip, the Emergency Medical Technician that was in the back with me kept an eye on my vital signs, but it was a reasonably quiet ride. Several times, I sent texts updating where we were along the way. I could see through the windows in the back of the ambulance, so I could tell where we were throughout the trip.

Unbeknownst to me, I was rolled into the delivery room when I arrived at the hospital. The doctor looked at me and asked if I was ready for my C-section, saying the baby would be born in about an hour. Immediately, I went into a panic —the first panic attack I had ever had—and my breathing became extremely labored. Imagine an elephant sitting on your chest while you are trying to breathe. Things went from calm with mid-nineties oxygen saturations to very rapid and shallow breaths and oxygen saturations in the eighties in a matter of a few minutes. I was alone, scared to death, and did I mention, *alone*!

I remember looking at the doctor and telling him "I'm

not here for a C-section! They told me I was coming to be monitored!" He quickly let me know "Yes ma'am, you *-are-* here for a C-section and you are very sick. We have to get this baby out so we can work on getting you better." At that point, I didn't know what had changed in my condition. They were trying their best to get the operating room ready, so it was never explained to me why they thought I needed to deliver right then. But, I also don't think it even crossed my mind to ask, either. I was more concerned with trying to catch my breath.

My first thoughts were that my family was at home under the impression that I was being monitored, but then the thought hit me that Baby E's parents were hours away and didn't know that their baby was about to be born. I asked the doctor if there was any way he could call the parents to let them know what was going on so that they could get on the road. He got their names and phone numbers from me. I texted Chris and my parents while the doctor called the baby's parents to let them know I would be giving birth soon. I was only thirty-four-and-a-half weeks pregnant, so they were still home in Alpharetta, Georgia.

Since Daddy lives closest to Savannah, he hopped in his truck and flew "Harris Airlines" (this is what I call his truck because he drove fast) to Savannah. God had his trip laid out. He didn't hit a single red light from Screven, Georgia, to the hospital. As soon as Daddy arrived, he was able to ask the questions we all had and to get answers. He was then able to explain to me what was happening and what needed to be done so that I could get well. Just his presence calmed me down a little bit. He made it just in time for the delivery, and he was able to video the birth and take pictures for the parents. At 11:39 p.m., Baby Eric was delivered via emergency cesarean section. He did very well and tested negative for

COVID (Although otherwise healthy, Eric spent ten days in Neonatal Intensive Care Unit because he was so early).

Rather than contaminate a recovery room, they let me recover in the operating room. At this point, I was back on high amounts of oxygen and still having trouble breathing. I was placed on a mask and that kept my levels at an acceptable level—not good, but acceptable.

Daddy was there because I had just come out of the operating room and he helped them get my bag and personal belongings moved to my room. I was moved to the fourth-floor COVID section and, again, no visitors were allowed, so as soon as I was settled into my room, my daddy had to leave. Now that he was headed back home, I began getting very nervous and agitated. At this point, I was twenty-five days post initial positive COVID test and was still testing positive. I had also just had my first C-section and was starting my recovery from that procedure.

My oxygen levels were still dropping with minimal movement, so I wasn't even allowed out of the bed to use the bathroom. The nurses would bring me a bed pan when I needed one. Many people might think I missed the baby during this time, but that was something I had prepared for because I had known the entire pregnancy that I would not have the baby after delivery. There were no 'baby blues' or depression after having him. I credit that to God, who prepared me for the day he would go with his parents— immediately after delivery—as happens even under the most ideal circumstances with surrogacy.

On Thursday, September 9th, one of the nurses took me downstairs to have a contrast CT scan, which would detect any blood clots. Before I went down, they had to get a twenty-gauge IV in my arm—above the elbow. I vividly remember them trying so hard to get it placed, but it took six or seven people before someone actually got it into a vein and it stayed. They ended up sticking me more than twenty times, and I had bruises up and down both arms. When the night shift nurse came on, she noticed I was post-partum, and my board said to do fundal massage. She looked at me and said, "I'm not sure what that means."

I, the non-healthcare professional, showed her, and she replied with "Oh! It looks like you're doing a pretty good job."

This made me nervous because I felt as if she was incapable of caring for me. I texted my family that they had to *immediately* get me off that floor. I had to be moved to where the staff would know how to take care of me. My hope was also to be on a floor that allowed visitors. What I didn't know at the time was that plans were already in the works to move me since I was more than twenty days post initial positive test and my condition was continuously worsening.

Mama was very good at calling and praying with me when my anxiety got bad or when my breathing was labored. With the increased anxiety, my breathing became faster and shallower. I would also get very nervous and begin worrying about everything, as my mind seemed to never stop racing. I remember feeling as if I could barely breathe and then feeling God's peace rush over me as soon as she started praying.

On Friday, September 10th, I was transferred to the cardiovascular ICU step-down unit. I knew that I was being moved, but I did not realize that I was in the ICU. I was also not aware of it at the time, but my condition was worsening. The Delta variant of COVID tended to begin by getting better, and then quickly going backward.

Once placed in the ICU, I was allowed one visitor-per hospital stay. Since Daddy had been there for Eric's delivery, he was the only one allowed with me. While this was tough for Mama and Chris, they knew that, with Daddy's flexible schedule and ability to calm me down, he was the best person to be there. Looking back, this was another moment in which God had things planned out before we had any idea of what was going on. He knew just who I needed to go to battle for me.

As my breathing worsened, I lay in bed begging God to give me breath. A few times, Daddy looked at my monitor and said, "Jess, you're breathing thirty-seven times per minute, and you need to be breathing more like fifteen or twenty. Let's try to calm down and breathe slower."

I sang "Great Are You, Lord" many times. I also had a cousin text me to say that she had been told to sing "Jesus Loves Me" anytime she got anxious, so I sang that a lot too.

The doctor prescribed Ativan to be given every four hours and hoped that once they got my anxiety under control, that I'd begin to get better, but I didn't.

During the weeks before, my cousin, Scott, was also diagnosed with COVID. He had been really sick and had made a few different trips to the hospital, fighting for his life. I believe that he was in the hospital when I went to Wayne Memorial in Jesup, and that he was placed on a ventilator. The morning before I transferred to Savannah, his sister messaged to check on me and I asked for an update on him. He had been taken off the ventilator and switched to the high-flow cannula. Although he had been taken off the vent, he was not waking up. As I was being transferred, Scott took a turn for the worse and had to be re-intubated.

The same morning that I was transferred to the cardio-vascular ICU step-down unit, Scott's sister messaged me again to let me know he had passed away. That was terrifying for me to hear. Although I didn't realize how sick I was becoming, I knew I was fighting the same virus that Scott had just died from. My family didn't want me to know about his death because they were worried about it upsetting me, but I knew before they did.

Saturday, September 11th, my son Kason turned five. I cried because I wasn't able to be with him that day, but my family did an excellent job celebrating him and FaceTiming me so that I could see him. They gave him a small birthday party and told me that as soon as I was home, we would have his actual party.

I was unaware of it then, but my body was no longer tolerating movement. My oxygen levels would drop and I would become pale. The doctor almost intubated me that day. I remember being asked about intubation, and I told the ICU doctor that was not what I wanted. The doctor thought I was asking for a do-not-resuscitate order (DNR), and I had to correct him and say that if it was absolutely necessary, to intubate me. But I carried no illusions. I had heard enough to know that if a person was intubated due to COVID, they had a very small chance of coming off the ventilator. It was also running through my mind that Scott had been intubated and had not survived.

I was limited on anxiety meds because they lowered my metabolism, which, in turn, would keep the high-flow oxygen from doing what I needed it to. The staff had to move me to another room twenty yards down the hall, into the ICU, and my oxygen saturation dropped to seventy-seven in the couple of minutes it took to roll my bed down the hall. The nurses had to unhook my oxygen tank to move me and they hadn't realized how quickly my numbers would drop. The doctors also discovered a blood clot in one of my lungs during the contrast CT and believed that was one of my most significant issues. Had it been any bigger, I would have been given the clot-buster shot that is given to stroke and heart attack patients, but they were concerned it would cause severe bleeding since I was only three days post-C-section. There had been a lot of changes in my stability in those three days, and I still had no idea that things were as bad as they were.

Saturday night, they rolled me over to put me on a bed pan and my oxygen dropped to sixty-eight, so Daddy told them that he wanted them to give me a catheter and that the doctor said to not move me anymore if my oxygen saturation dropped like that again. At one point that night, I lay in bed and audibly cried out to God to put air in my lungs and allow me to breathe. I repeated "God, please give me breath" over and over. It was the single most terrifying thing that I have ever experienced.

## 5

## RESPIRATORY AND CARDIAC ARREST

"FOR I AM CONVINCED THAT NEITHER DEATH NOR LIFE,
NEITHER ANGELS NOR DEMONS, NEITHER THE PRESENT
NOR THE FUTURE, NOR ANY POWERS, NEITHER HEIGHT NOR
DEPTH, NOR ANYTHING ELSE IN ALL CREATION, WILL BE
ABLE TO SEPARATE US FROM THE LOVE OF GOD THAT IS IN
CHRIST JESUS, OUR LORD" (ROMANS 8:38-39).

Around 3:30 on Sunday morning, September 12th, I called my mama and told her that I could not breathe and asked her to please pray for me. I remember that she, Fred, and Chris gathered together in our driveway and called my great aunt and uncle to pray with me over the phone. I was finally able to calm down enough to fall asleep for a little while. That is the last thing that I remember until about fifteen days later after I awoke from my coma. But I've been able to piece together the life I lived during those fifteen days through texts sent by my daddy and the stories my family and caretakers have told me.

By 8:30 that Sunday morning, the hospital had called Daddy and told him that I was getting worse fast and that they would be putting me on the ventilator within the hour. Daddy left church and rushed to Savannah. He talked with the doctor and nurses, and they decided that they had no choice but to intubate me.

. . .

*It breaks my heart to read the notes from these days that were so agonizing for my family. Daddy told Chris and the rest of our loved ones, "I am here holding her hand."*

*Reading these texts that say, "Please tell her that I love her." Brings me to tears every time.*

Daddy had been sent to the waiting room while they prepared to intubate me. He heard them call the code over the intercom but did not realize that it was me who had coded until the nurse came out and laid her hand on his arm. The parents of the baby that I'd carried were in the NICU visiting him and also heard the code over the intercom. They recall looking at each other and saying, "It can't be her!"

At noon, Daddy sent a message to the family that read "Y'all be praying hard right now. I will get back with you as soon as I can. I am back here with her. She went into cardiac arrest. They brought her back and are working on her. I will call when I can."

I died. COVID killed me.

After my cardiac arrest, doctors considered the clot-buster shot again, but they were afraid that it would cause a stroke. My cardiac arrest lasted somewhere between six and ten minutes, but once again, God had things laid out.

My medical team had seen enough to know that, as a postpartum patient, my heart would likely stop when they intubated me. Hence, they had the crash team there waiting to begin CPR. They were unsure if there would be brain damage due to my heart being stopped for so long. Still, they did an excellent job of keeping the oxygen moving through me with a manual resuscitator (Ambu bag) for more than two hours and by starting CPR immediately. The doctor started me on a medicine called Flolan, which increases pulmonary arterial flow, or blood flow, to the lungs, and decreases pulmonary pressures. This helped to improve the gas exchange (carbon dioxide for oxygen) and thus arterial oxygenation, allowing them to stop bagging me.

The doctors allowed my step-mom to come up and stay with Daddy for the rest of the day. They also let Daddy remain with me that night even though visiting hours ended at six p.m. During this time, a chaplain from the hospital came to see Daddy and prayed with him. He would continue to visit up until my discharge. That day, my life was very touch and go.

I found out later that three women were asked by God to stay up Sunday night and pray for me the entire time. Many churches had special prayers during their services for me. I know of five churches that had someone stand for me during prayer. These people either stood or knelt at the altar at their church while the congregation gathered around, laid hands on the person, and prayed for my healing.

# 6

## ECMO

EVEN THOUGH I WALK THROUGH THE DARKEST VALLEY, I
WILL FEAR NO EVIL, FOR YOU ARE WITH ME; YOUR ROD AND
YOUR STAFF, THEY COMFORT ME" (PSALMS 23:4).

*M*y chest x-rays looked pretty bad, and the doctor started discussing Extracorporeal Membrane Oxygenation (ECMO) with Daddy and my step-mom. Palliative care had also been called in to speak with Daddy and discuss my condition and the ECMO cannulation (placement of tubing).

Sunday night's update from Daddy was pretty grim. It said, "OK. The ICU doctor just came in. Our girl is very sick. If she had been anywhere but a hospital, she wouldn't have made it. If she had been 20-30 years older, she would not have made it. Her youth is on her side. She is still deep in the woods and this thing can go either way. She is a fighter though and she will fight through this. According to him, the ultrasound helped him determine that all of this is due to extreme COVID pneumonia. Her lungs are not in good shape at all. It is going to be a journey. The blood clot could have contributed but it is not a huge clot. It is more from the COVID. She basically had respiratory arrest because of the COVID pneumonia which in turn sent her into cardiac arrest. We need her to fight. There is a good chance that they will put her on an ECMO machine. That will be so that her organs can rest and her blood still gets oxygenated and pushes good blood to all of her organs. So, pray that our girl fights for her life and fights for the will to live. It is day by day. She is considered very critical right now. She is on three blood pressure drugs to try to control her blood pressure. Her Flolan meds are helping her really well. This is the latest as I know it."

Sunday night, the food started coming in for my family from people throughout our extended family and community. My cousin Scott's family was gathered and had more food than they could eat, so they even brought food over to feed my family.

On Monday, September 13th, the decision was made to put me on ECMO. This was the last "hail mary" to save me. I was placed on venovenous ECMO, which is where they inserted a cannula (tube) in my internal right jugular vein in my neck that drained the blood from my body. It was then pumped through the ECMO machine, which took the carbon dioxide out of the blood and re-oxygenated it and then put it back into my body via a cannula in the right internal femoral vein in the groin.

The update from Daddy read, "This is the last thing that can be done to save Jess as far as medical procedures are concerned. If this doesn't work, and if the Lord doesn't see fit to step in, Jess will not survive this COVID pneumonia."

Text messages poured into my phone and my family members' phones. Prayers were going up all over the world. At last count, people from forty different countries were calling out my name to the Ultimate Healer and begging for His healing.

While on ECMO, I had a dedicated ICU nurse as well as a dedicated cardiovascular perfusionist. These perfusionists operate the ECMO machine and monitor the patient around the clock.

That night, after Chris let his parents know what was happening and how things were looking, his mom, Andrea, flew down from Illinois. She had gone to work that morning, but when she got the call about ECMO being the last resort, her boss sent her home and told her to take care of her family. Immediately, a flight was booked and she headed to Georgia. She stayed through Friday and helped with the boys, meals, and anything else that needed to be done. My family has repeatedly said she was a blessing to them during such difficult days.

Tuesday, September 14th, was a rough day. My lungs took a step in the wrong direction. The ICU doctor told Daddy, at that point in time, that only one patient who had COVID and had been put on ECMO had survived at their hospital. Daddy said to him that he was looking at *Number Two*. I am still known as "Number Two" to this day.

Daddy was also told it was not uncommon for the lungs to continue to digress the first day after ECMO initiation. Daddy recorded a video of the doctor telling my family that I was in very critical condition and that my chances of survival were very slim. No one saw the video until after I came home. Mama remembers getting the news and leaning over in her chair, holding her face in her hands. She said she heard the back door to her house open and then felt someone rubbing her back; it was Andrea, Chris's mom.

A lady from my church posted this on Facebook Tuesday afternoon: "In a culture that has devalued the lives of unborn babies daily, I have the greatest admiration for this precious lady, Jessica, who made such a great sacrifice to give life to a baby and to give the gift of parenting to a couple who might not have had it otherwise. Sadly, she now has

COVID and is fighting for her own life. Please pray fervently for a miracle of healing in her lungs so that she can come home to her own precious family. We know God can heal her with one touch, and selfishly, I pray for that healing to be for life and health for Jess. His ways are not our ways and we trust in His goodness no matter what the outcome is. But right now, it sure would bring rejoicing and gladness to so many hearts if she could come back to her family and be restored.

"Please, Dear Lord, raise her body like You did for the daughter of Jairus. You took her by the hand and said, 'My child, get up.' Her spirit returned, and she was raised up to life again. There was also Lazarus, and numerous others. We trust in You completely, Lord, and we give You thanks in advance for her healing, in whatever way You choose. Please also give Your sweet presence and power to all of her family during these days of waiting."

This is just one of the many, many prayers you will find if you scroll through my or my family's Facebook pages during my eight weeks in the hospital.

My step-daddy, Fred, received a text from Mr. Robbie, a co-worker of his who is a pastor outside his job with Coca-Cola. The text read, "I want y'all to listen to this old song [he sent a YouTube link]. Only three times in my ministry has the Lord told me to tell somebody that it's going to be ok. TODAY IS THE THIRD TIME!!!!! I want you to do something. I want you, Debra [my mama] and Jessica's dad to hold hands together and accept the miracle and thank the Lord for what He is about to do!!! We love you and your family."

My mama, daddy, and stepdad did what Mr. Robbie asked them to do. Within two hours, the doctor told them that my chance of survival at that point was "slim to none."

My family struggled so much and did everything they could to just hold it together. My husband had to be Mama and Daddy. His wife had died and been brought back, and he didn't know if I would make it back home or not. Our boys were five, twelve, and fourteen, and they were extremely close to losing their mama. My parents were left wondering if their daughter would ever come home. My brother almost became their only biological child.

After this message from Mr. Robbie, God spoke to Mama. She put this thought in her notes: "We BELIEVE God has been with Jessica all this time, but we also believe that God let the doctors do all they could do and THEN HE STEPPED IN BECAUSE HE WAS NOT DONE WITH JESSICA here on Earth and we needed a miracle that only He could give."

# 7

## VICTORY CLAIMED

"WHEN HE HEARD THIS, JESUS SAID, 'THIS SICKNESS WILL
NOT END IN DEATH. NO, IT IS FOR GOD'S GLORY SO THAT
GOD'S SON MAY BE GLORIFIED THROUGH IT" (JOHN 11:4).

*W*ednesday, September 15th, Daddy claimed my victory over COVID. My arterial blood gasses had improved, and my lungs also showed slight improvement. The last part of his update that morning was "Fight, baby, fight, and I will be so glad when I take you home." He also started my slogan that day: *"She is one day closer to going home."*

It was planned that they would give me a tracheotomy, that day, to get the tube out of my throat. The trach was to be put in because it was more beneficial to use as a long-term breathing machine than the vent tube in my mouth, including a decreased chance of infection since my mouth would then be able to close. However, an emergency arose and the doctor had to postpone it until the next day. My church brought a van full of people and held a prayer vigil outside the hospital that evening.

Chest x-rays showed more improvement Thursday morning. God was showing what He was capable of doing! Daddy reminded *Dr. Russia*, my pulmonologist and one of the ICU doctors, that I was going to be Number Two. Daddy called him Dr. Russia because he was from Russia and Daddy couldn't spell nor pronounce his name, Dr. Aksenov.

Chris and Mama were allowed to visit for an hour after my trach surgery Thursday afternoon. Chris remembers seeing three IV poles with thirteen bags of medications hanging on each pole that stood next to my bedside while he was there.

Friday, September 17th, brought more improvement, but my hemoglobin began dropping. Hemoglobin is a protein in the red blood cells, which carries oxygen through your body. If the hemoglobin drops, your body no longer gets the required oxygen. Prayers continued to flood the gates of heaven on my behalf. The obstetricians came in to check my bleeding from the delivery (I was only nine days postpartum, so some bleeding was expected.) Of course, I was on blood thinners from the blood clot and ECMO, which worsened my bleeding. Daddy also began planning my first church service back at church that day. My family was claiming God's victory!

Saturday, September 18th, came with a little more improvement regarding my blood pressure. My lungs stayed about the same, but the doctors were pleased with *status quo* every once in a while. They'd dropped the oxygen level on my ECMO machine to seventy percent, and my oxygen saturation was remaining at one hundred percent.

Uncle Terry (Daddy's brother) called from Belize that day and prayed over me. Daddy also had a great conversation with one of my perfusionists (the individual who runs the ECMO machine). He was the perfusionist who, along with the cardiothoracic surgeon, decided that I was a good candidate for ECMO. He told Daddy that he had a feeling that I would make it and that my team *needed* me to make it. You wouldn't believe the toll it takes on doctors, nurses, perfusionists, respiratory therapists, and physical therapists —to lose patient after patient. They needed a win.

By Sunday, September 19th, they had lowered the oxygen on my ECMO to forty percent. That was a HUGE step in the right direction because they were hoping to get to sixty percent by Monday.

## 8

---

## WAKING UP

"I LIE DOWN AND SLEEP; I WAKE AGAIN, BECAUSE THE LORD
SUSTAINS ME." (PSALMS 3:5)

*M*onday, September 20<sup>th</sup>, the ECMO was lowered to thirty-five percent oxygen. I get tickled when I read Daddy's update from that night. He starts off, "Welllllllll, GGGGLLLLOOOORRRYYY!!!!!!"

I began waking up enough to respond to Daddy when he talked to me! He asked questions, and I would slightly shake my head to acknowledge what he said. He told me what had happened, where I was, and that they needed me to keep fighting! He called Chris, the boys, Mama, Mallory (my sister-in-law), Emmaline (my niece), Jaxon (my nephew), my step-mom, and Karla (my step-sister) and let them talk to me.

I heard them!!!

In my mind, I was in a fish tank at Addictive Aquatics, a local fish and pet store from home. Matt and Krystal, the owners, were with me holding my hands while I heard my family tell me that I was going to be okay and that they loved me.

During the night on Monday, the doctors put me back on sedation and paralytic medicine because I was trying to move too much, negatively affecting my oxygen saturation levels. Still, they were pleased with the neurological signs that I had shown while waking up. At this point, the doctors were still not sure if there would be any brain damage from the lapsed time during my cardiac arrest, but they were optimistic.

It really is amazing—the crazy, vivid dreams that you have while you are in a coma! I remember two in particular, and one seemed to last a few days. It was very long and seemingly real. The long one actually happened after I came out of the coma because I called Kaleb and Chris in the middle of the night, and my nurse had to take my phone away until morning. I am not really sure why I called because my tracheotomy prevented me from talking. The phone call was only one thing that happened during that wakeful dream, but for now, I'll only share the real details.

On Tuesday, September 21$^{st}$, Daddy thought they had decided to begin the process of taking me off of ECMO, and that they planned to do it either Wednesday or Thursday, but he misunderstood what they meant. The doctors were able to lower the oxygen on the ECMO machine to twenty-one percent, which is what we breathe normally, and turned the ventilator to fifty percent. Daddy continued to close out each update with my slogan: *She is one day closer to coming home!*

Wednesday morning, September 22$^{nd}$, we were told I wouldn't be taken off ECMO, but that they would be switching out my cannulas. I had one cannula in my groin and another in my neck. I was put on what is called an Avalon cannula, which takes the groin cannula out and moves everything to the neck. The Avalon cannula was new to Memorial Health. By moving the groin cannula, the staff could take me off paralytic medicines, sit me up, and get me moving a little bit. Moving around would help the fluid in my lungs begin to move out and help me recover strength in my muscles that had deteriorated while unable to move. This proved to be an excellent decision, and I responded to treatment really well after that surgery.

Thursday, September 23$^{rd}$, was another good day. Prayers were being answered! I had some visitors from some of the top people in the hospital because I was the first patient at Memorial Health in over ten years to pull through what I had been through so far and to recover at such a good rate. When a patient needs ECMO, they are the most critical patients in the hospital. It is not unusual for ECMO patients to pass away either while on the life support or soon after being de-cannulated. I'm not sure what criteria I met to make me that one patient to reach that goal, but that's what they told Daddy. The first piece of history that I wrote at Memorial Health University Medical Center was about some of my recovery experiences.

The physical therapists came by to see me and were impressed with the strength I had. The doctors also came in and tried what is called a 'trach collar' that day (Thursday). A trach collar is separate from the ventilator. It pushes oxygen through the trach from the regular oxygen connection in the room's wall. More history here; this made me the first patient to ever be taken off of the ventilator while still on ECMO. I feel certain this is just Memorial's statistics.

I seemed to tolerate the trach collar well, but was put back on the ventilator so that I could rest and continue healing. I did get to stay on the trach collar for two hours, though, which was a big deal to me. I asked if I could Face-Time Chris that day and was able to see him some while he was at work. That did us both a lot of good.

After seeing the continued improvement from being

switched to the Avalon cannula, the doctor asked Daddy if they could bring another patient's wife in to look at the cannula. She wanted to see it before making the decision to change her husband to that cannula.

Friday, September 24th, was kind of a chill day. I had had two big days with the ECMO surgery on Wednesday and the trach collar trial on Thursday, so I rested most of Friday. Physical therapy did come in and work with me a good bit that day doing some leg exercises in the bed, which also wore me out. The therapists also brought me a ball to throw to practice my reflexes. Speech therapy came and put a speaking valve in my trach, which allowed me to talk to Daddy a little bit and tell them how I was feeling. It was so strange to be able to speak again! It was also a relief to know that the tracheotomy tube had not affected my voice. Talking through the trach was not as easy as you may think, so the lady from speech therapy had to coach me on how to speak with it. Moving around also helped break up a lot of the fluid from my lungs, but that meant that I had to cough a lot of that up, and the nurses suctioned my trach a lot, making me really tired.

Friday night or early Saturday morning, I started bleeding too much from my uterus again. At the time, they were able to keep it under control, but planned to keep a close eye on it.

My poor Daddy had to have a challenging conversation with me that day after I asked where I was. It was emotional for him, but he told me about the cardiac arrest and every-thing else that had occurred. Daddy felt it was best to be honest with me just as he had asked the doctors to be honest with him. Sugar-coating it would not help anyone and he didn't want to give me false hope. He told me that I was a miracle, but that I still had a lot of work to do.

The speaking valve for the trach was only there for a short time because the ventilator could not be hooked up with the valve in. Because of this, Daddy worked with me a lot on communication since I couldn't talk. We worked a lot on lip-reading, and Daddy got really good at it, but sometimes, he just had no idea what I was trying to say, so we started working on writing. The most challenging part of writing was my lack of strength, which made it hard to hold the pen. Keep in mind that I was still on ECMO with a huge cannula coming out of my neck. That cannula also was the outlet/inlet for all of the blood in my body, so I couldn't move my neck at all to be able to see what or where I was writing. I was able to write for the first time on Saturday, September 25th. The first thing I wrote was "Where's Chris?"

Sunday was spent continuing to work on communication. We spent time writing and using my phone again. I was able to get into my pictures to show my nurses some of the tumblers I had made. I also tried to send text messages. Daddy told people to send me short text messages so I could start communicating with them. He reminded them that I was extremely far-sighted and that if my glasses were not on, I would not be able to read their messages, so it could take time to respond.

Sunday night, I got my hair washed for the first time in almost a month by some of my nurses and my perfusionist. The perfusionist had to be very careful due to the ECMO cannula in my neck. I couldn't move my head much at all so that the cannula wouldn't move. They also had to wash carefully because I had a lot of blood matted in my hair from the ECMO cannula and the trach-site bleeding. You do not realize how complex the most minor tasks can be for a critical patient until you go through something like this. Having my hair washed was absolutely amazing. I've always enjoyed having someone play with my hair. You would think my head would itch from my hair being dirty, but I don't remember any itching. Afterward, Shelby, one of the nurses, braided my hair.

Sunday night was also the night that they took my phone away, so it must have been the last night of that very long dream where I called Kaleb and Chris.

I had a central line in my neck, and that was taken out on Monday, September $27^{th}$, and a peripherally inserted central catheter (PICC line) was placed in my arm. The PICC line would help decrease the chance of infection and was just better all around. Physical therapy also came in and helped me sit up in bed. Daddy reminded the rest of the family that, while I was making HUGE progress, I was still on two forms of life support and had to have both to survive. I needed my lungs to heal and to maintain a minimum oxygen saturation of seventy percent to survive. The doctors, however, were finally feeling like I would walk out of the hospital on my own.

Uncle Terry called again that day and talked to me on speaker phone. I tried to relay a message to him, but Daddy couldn't understand me, so he got my notepad. I wrote, "I'm showing them what a Harris can do!"

Ti
I'm seeing then

What a Harris

Can do!

# 9

# SITTING AND STANDING UP

"I CAN DO ALL THINGS THROUGH CHRIST WHO
STRENGTHENS ME" (PHILIPPIANS 4:13).

On Tuesday, September 28th, history was made again. I sat up while on ECMO! This was quite the feat! For me to sit or stand, a perfusionist had to hold the ECMO tubes in place behind me. There was also at least one nurse, a respiratory therapist, and three physical therapists there to make sure everything went as planned. I also wanted a hairbrush because my hair was a *mess*. My nurses were so wonderful and found a comb to try to work out some of the tangles in the back of my head. Although they had washed and braided my hair a few nights before, getting the matted hair untangled proved to be a challenge, but I happily dealt with the tugs and pulls at my scalp.

Very early in my illness, my family started ministering to the hospital staff by bringing snacks and treats daily. People would come from other floors to get a snack. "Feed them and they will come."

On this particular day, an operating room nurse came up to see me and said that, on her floor, they would talk about the lady on the fifth floor and how well she was doing and that her daddy always brought the best treats.

Two people from physical therapy who didn't work with me came up to see the video of me sitting up. They were all amazed at my progress.

Another historical event occurred was made on Wednesday, September 29th, when I was the first patient to stand up while on ECMO! My room was *full* of people who wanted to see it first-hand. Daddy had Chris on FaceTime while I stood, so he could watch me in real time rather than waiting for the video to be sent via text message.

## 10

## BLEEDING ISSUES

"AND WHEN I PASSED BY YOU AND SAW YOU STRUGGLING
IN YOUR OWN BLOOD, I SAID TO YOU IN YOUR BLOOD, 'LIVE!'
YES, I SAID TO YOU IN YOUR BLOOD, 'LIVE!'" (EZEKIEL 16:6).

*D*uring this time of huge strides, I was still bleeding a lot. They took me to surgery and did a uterine arterial embolization to attempt to stop the bleeding. Being on the ventilator and ECMO, I had a lot of equipment that had to be taken to the operating room with me. It took four or five people to get me and my medical equipment from one place to the next. This was no small task. During my trip to and from the operating room, my vent tube got caught on door handles as we passed through the small hallways. It didn't hurt or pull my trach loose when it got caught because we noticed immediately, but it was a funny story.

I was allowed to stay awake during the procedure, and it hurt pretty badly. My pain tolerance is usually pretty high, so I never said anything to them about the pain: I just lay there and winced. Pain blockers were given, but I could still feel pain throughout the procedure. This was one of only two times I remember being in significant pain during my hospital stay. Blessedly, I recovered well from the surgery and got some good rest.

Thursday, September 30th, was another chill day, given to me so that I could rest from the recent surgery. Daddy trimmed my fingernails so I could get to the keyboard on my phone. The text messages began! I loved hearing from my family. Daddy and I found out that they were trying to get permission for my boys to come see me and that made me cry. I had not been able to see them in a month and my mama-heart needed my babies. The problem was that children under twelve were not allowed in the hospital. I wanted to see my boys, but I wanted to see *all* my boys. After missing Kason's birthday, I especially wanted to see him.

During this time, I had a visit from one of the respiratory therapy guys who was with me when I went into cardiac arrest. He said he wanted to see the miracle and said that when he was doing CPR on me, I'd only had a ten percent chance of living. It was nice to meet those who were with me during such a devastating time. At the same time, hearing how critical I had been was difficult.

Physical therapy didn't come that day because they wanted me to recover from surgery and hopefully stop bleeding. Thursday night, I started bleeding pretty badly again. I had a very extensive ultrasound, and they recommended a hysterectomy. But I had already had a lot of blood transfusions (by the end of my hospital stay, I received fifty-four units of blood) and continuing to give me transfusions wouldn't have been good for my lungs. I was okay with the hysterectomy, as my family was complete and I didn't have any plans to attempt another surrogacy.

Around lunch on Friday, the doctor came in and talked to me and Daddy. This was probably the most scared I had been since waking up from the coma. My bleeding had gotten worse, and they were having trouble stopping it. I had a device called a Bakri balloon (a Bakri balloon puts pressure on the inside of the uterus) inserted to try to slow the bleeding. It helped a little, but then the bleeding started back up again. My blood was not clotting like it should. Because of this, they told us I would not survive a hysterectomy. If they didn't get the bleeding to stop, I would bleed to death. It was terrifying to think that I had come so far in my recovery from COVID and yet was so close to dying from internal bleeding. My blood thinners were turned off again, and they decided to try a procedure called Manual Uterine Aspiration (MUA) which means that they manually removed clots from my uterus. They also placed something called Surgiflo™ in my uterus in an attempt to seal off any bleeding areas.

Through this time, my papa's friend told my family to recite Ezekiel 16:6 three times as a prayer and to put my name in it. "I passed by you and saw you thrashing around in your blood, and I said to you as you lay in your blood, 'Live!' Yes, I said to you as you lay in your blood, 'Live!'" He told them to lay hands on me, which they could not do, so they did the next best thing and laid hands on a picture of me. After three to four hours of being off blood thinners, the bleeding had slowed to almost a complete stop. They let me stay off the blood thinners for a couple more hours, but had to turn them back on so that the ECMO could work like it was supposed to. They began working to get me off ECMO. If that didn't work, they had two other options to try before resorting to the hysterectomy.

# KAMERON'S TEXT

"BLESSED ARE THE PURE IN HEART, FOR THEY SHALL SEE
GOD" (MATTHEW 5:8).

*D*ue to all the bleeding and trouble I had sleeping, I missed a text from my son, Kameron on Friday morning, October 1st. God spoke to my boy. His message read, "I know you are probably asleep, but if you read this in the morning, I want you to know that you will be ok, and I honestly feel that, in the end, you will be alright. We have been bent down to our knees, and God picked you back up and told you and everybody else to fight hard and pray hard. And we have been, but we are going to fight harder and pray harder, and I believe that we will all make it through this long journey and this bumpy road will go on to be a smooth road. No matter how many bumpy roads, it will come to a smooth road.

"And we have been thinking about it. If it were us, we wouldn't have made it as far as you, and God is doing this for you to prove the world wrong and that He is King. He has made you come this far. He will not forget or give up on you. He needs you to do a big thing in this world, and I am telling you, you will be a miracle, and people will be jealous of us, and mainly you, for how much God has done through you. He knew what He was going to do when you were born, and He has talked to me in these past few weeks, and we have all gotten closer to Him in the journey.

"We love you and we will do whatever He wants us to do to get you home because He needs you to do something. Your name will be world-wide and everybody will pray until you get better. And when you do, we will all be thanking God for touching you and for laying His hand on your heart. I LOVE YOU, MAMA!"

In the words of my Uncle Lynn, "If that doesn't light your fire, your wood's wet."

Around this time, Mama and Fred started calling me each night and praying with me. I was still unable to talk, so we would text prior to the call and they would ask what specific things I needed prayers for that night. We had a rule that once they prayed, if I was okay, I would hang the phone up and go to bed. They called me every night for the remainder of my hospital stay and prayed for me and anyone else on their prayer list. I still had some bleeding during the night Friday and early Saturday morning. Still, it was significantly less than Friday afternoon, so the new procedure they tried helped. I still had to have a procedure that day to try to get the bleeding to stop completely. They put something similar to a gel-foam in my uterus and then put the Bakri balloon back in.

# 12

# COMING OFF ECMO

"I SOUGHT THE LORD AND HE HEARD ME, AND DELIVERED
ME FROM ALL MY FEARS" (PSALMS 34:4).

*T*he doctors began weaning me off ECMO. By the time Daddy left, I was only getting thirty percent pure oxygen from ECMO and could dispel carbon dioxide entirely on my own. The blood thinners were turned off again and the blood that was in my catheter was clotted! The doctors came in and talked to us about me being put on the lung transplant list. They had seen a lot of scarring on my lungs and felt that a double lung transplant might be necessary. After our discussion, they got the ball rolling and put me on the transplant list with Emory University Hospital in Atlanta. That was one of the toughest conversations I remember—that and the hysterectomy conversation.

The research Daddy did following the transplant conversation showed life expectancy after a lung transplant to be about five years, so that was not the best long-term solution. I was much better off working on getting my lungs to a place where they could sustain my life on their own. My lungs were showing improvement, but were still extremely scarred from COVID pneumonia, so weaning from ECMO did not mean that I didn't need the transplant anymore. The doctors were afraid that my lungs may not be able to keep my body oxygenated long-term.

At 11:30 Sunday morning, October 3, 2021, one of my cardiothoracic surgeons, Dr. Stouffer, came in and asked, "Are you ready?"

After I'd been on ECMO for twenty-one days, he took me off! It was an eerie feeling as the cannula was removed. That had been my life-line for the last twenty-one days. Also, with such a large hole in such a major vein, Dr. Stouffer had to hold pressure on the site for almost thirty minutes.

The lady I had the baby for said that her cousin, who is a doctor, said in response to a text saying I'd come off ECMO: "The best ECMO is no ECMO!"

Shortly after ECMO was shut off, I started running a low-grade fever, which was expected since ECMO kept my blood temperature lower than the normal 98.6 degrees.

My team planned to start me back up with physical therapy and decided to take the Bakri balloon out of my uterus to see if the bleeding had stopped. The biggest prayer at that time was that my lungs would be able to control my blood gases on their own and that they would continue to improve so that I could stay off ECMO. I was ready to get back home!

I don't remember it well, but there was another patient in the ICU whose wife visited him every day. She had to pass my room to get to his, and she would wave at me as she passed. One day, she stopped, asked why I was there, and told me and Daddy about her husband. She told me that she was praying for me, too. Daddy assured her that we would be praying for her husband as well. I am not sure what happened with her husband, but I do know that he was airlifted to Emory University Hospital in Atlanta for surgery.

She brought their son by to see me on their way out on their last day there.

Daddy's Monday morning update said, "Well, I walked into a room with a bright-eyed blonde grinning from ear to ear this morning, listening to a doctor say 'this is simply a miracle.' She is doing really well, and it appears that her bleeding has stopped. She is completely off of ECMO and is almost on the lowest setting of the ventilator." He ended again with "She is one day closer to going home." Monday turned out to be the best day I'd had in a long time and I was able to try the speaking valve again.

When physical therapy came Tuesday morning, October 5th, I was able to get up and walk to the chair and sit in it. I was able to tolerate the movement and maintain my oxygen saturations. My temperature had started dropping and my heart rate and blood pressure were really good. We also got the approval for Chris, Kaleb, Kameron, *and Kason* to come up the next day. I spent a couple of hours in the recliner and watched TV most of that day.

The physical therapists put me in the recliner on Wednesday morning (October 6th, 2021) so that I would be better able to interact with the boys when they got there. Kason was scared to touch me due to the IV lines, the trach, and the feeding tube. Daddy had to reassure him that I was okay and that he could hug me. It had been thirty-six days since I had laid eyes on my boys. I cried as they stood around me.

A lady from Child Life Services soon came in to help the boys understand what was going on with the equipment and gave them a kit to make bracelets and necklaces for themselves and me. They drew some pictures, and she had a quilt for them to give to me. We spent a couple hours with each other, which did my heart some good. All in all, it was a great visit, but boy was it hard to watch them walk out that door, not knowing when I would see them again.

That night, the respiratory therapists moved some of my ventilator settings and were able to set the *peep* to six. The peep is the amount of pressure that a ventilator uses to push the air into a person's lungs. After determining to spend some time in the recliner, I was pretty much able to sit up in the bed by myself and stand up with a bit of help getting started. I stayed in the chair for a few hours, but had to get back in bed for an abdominal x-ray. I had developed an air pocket at the base of my feeding tube, which caused some nausea. (One thing no one thinks about with trach patients is how they throw up. Let me assure you it is neither pretty nor fun.)

We discussed changing my feeding tube to a percutaneous endoscopic gastrostomy (PEG) tube, but they ultimately decided to keep the nasogastric (NG) tube. The PEG would have been inserted through my abdomen and directly into my stomach instead of the NG tube in my nose. I absolutely HATED that NG tube. It got in my way all the time. I would even venture to say that the NG tube was worse than the ECMO lines and the trach.

On Friday, October 8th, I was able to stand up by myself. I got my vent tube caught on the bed and pulled it loose. It was a great "breathing trial," as the physical therapist said. It all worked out fine.

The doctors started talking to us about in-patient rehab, and we discussed the places I could go. It all made me uncomfortable because I knew I wouldn't be allowed visitors except for a couple of hours per day, and I knew it would be crazy for someone to drive two hours just to stay a couple of hours and then go home.

Saturday, October 9th, they dropped pressure support,

which helped decrease the work my lungs had to do to inflate, on the vent from twenty-four to twenty. The goal was to get it to ten and then they would start the trach collar again, allowing me to breathe on my own through the trach, pushing pure oxygen through it rather than room air. It is a hose that comes from the oxygen that comes from a regular tank instead of a ventilator. Sunday morning, October 10th, the ICU doctor said to wait to start the trach collar, but my favorite respiratory therapist, Ken, decided to try it anyway. I wore it for twenty minutes and I maintained my oxygen saturation. The doctor was amazed when he was told how well I'd done. They decided to try it for an hour on and three hours off the next day. That was an excellent start to getting me off the vent and ready to go to the rehabilitation center.

Monday morning, October 11th, the pressure on the vent was lowered to sixteen. I tolerated that move well. I restarted blood thinners, continuing to work on the blood clot in my lungs. At the same time, doctors carefully monitored me for bleeding.

Starting blood thinners again was very stressful. I prayed so hard that I wouldn't start bleeding again. I did pass a couple of blood clots that day, but nothing anyone was concerned about. It still scared me, though. I did well on the trach collar that day and had three sessions of an hour each on it.

On Tuesday, we did a two-hour run with the collar on. After a three-hour break, we started the collar again. When those two hours were up, I was doing well and my oxygen was saturating where I needed it to be, so they left it on. We started talking about Landmark, the rehab center, again.

My white blood count started rising Wednesday morning, October 13th, so the doctors took a couple of different cultures to find out what was going on, and I was given a generic antibiotic until the cultures came back. The elevated white blood count meant that there was some type of infection somewhere in my body; thus, the cultures to try to find the infection. They also lowered the pressure support on the vent to ten, but I didn't tolerate a jump that big very well, so it was bumped back up some. One of my cardiothoracic surgeons, Dr. Willekes, came to visit and said they were using me as a model for future patients. Dr. Willekes also said he had great contacts at Landmark and that he would let them know that I was one of his VIPs. He also assured us that they would take good care of me there.

When Daddy would leave for the night, my anxiety started to ramp up, and I got to where I couldn't sleep. I would stay awake all night watching television. I wouldn't be surprised if I watched every episode of *The Golden Girls* during those nights. If I'm not mistaken, I also watched *Frazier* a good bit. I believe the anxiety stemmed from my fear of going to the rehab center and being alone again. My hospital room was right next to the helipad, so I also heard all the flights coming in and out of the hospital, which kept me awake, too. On top of that, I was also near the children's hospital. One night, I recall lying in bed and listening to them call a code blue to the pediatric floor. I will never forget that call. My heart sank when they said it was for the children's hospital.

## 13

# WALKING AROUND

"SO THE MULTITUDE MARVELED WHEN THEY SAW THE
MUTE SPEAKING, THE MAIMED MADE WHOLE, THE LAME
WALKING, AND THE BLIND SEEING; AND THEY GLORIFIED
THE GOD OF ISRAEL" (MATTHEW 15:31).

*T*hursday, October 14, 2021, the doctors began treating me like they do babies and made me stay awake during the day so that I would sleep at night. My hemoglobin levels started dropping again, meaning I was losing blood, therefore not getting oxygenated like I needed. I had to have more blood transfusions.

I was able to get up and walk down the hall that day, and I think that was a good pick-me-up for everyone. The entire staff was excited and clapped for me. One of my physical therapy girls even cried while we were walking.

While I made some significant strides in my recovery, things at home were not going as well. Chris and Justin had gotten into an altercation and that put a strain on me emotionally. It felt like I was being forced to choose between my husband and my brother, and that also caused some arguments between me and Chris. The arguments frustrated me because I was fighting to stay alive, and being pulled into the middle of family drama in which I didn't need to be involved. There were a few other incidents during my hospital stay that didn't sit quite right with me, and caused some strain on my marriage.

Staying awake all day Thursday allowed me to sleep that night, so Daddy kept me awake all day Friday as well. They never determined what caused the drop in my hemoglobin levels or the elevated white blood counts, but both improved with antibiotics, blood transfusions, and lots of prayers. I was able to spend six hours in the trach collar during the night. Daddy recorded me saying, "Hey y'all! I can't wait to see you again!" I got a little teary trying to say it. I was so, so ready to see my family again. It ended up that I was able to spend nine hours in the trach collar that day.

*She is one day closer to coming home!*

Of course, nurses change as the shift changes, but there are also multiple nurses who work the ICU, so I rotated through quite a few. Most of them were my nurse for several days, but there were a few who I only had once or twice. Those that I had more often, obviously, became closer to me and Daddy the more shifts they spent with us. To this day, I remember most of their names and can name them in pictures.

I don't remember when Gaby started being my nurse, but she was an absolute hoot! She and Daddy got along very well, and they both loved to talk, so there were many conversations between the two of them. One that I will never forget was about the PureWick™ external catheter. This catheter is used in place of a foley catheter, which is inserted into the urethra. An external catheter is also a step above a bed pan. It hooks to the suction in the wall, and a cotton wick held in collection tubing fits up between your legs. You pee into it, and it suctions the urine into a canister. Daddy had asked for it because I needed to use the bathroom, and Gaby told him that she called the PureWick™ a "cooter canoe." (If you've ever heard my daddy laugh, it's very loud, and you can pick him out of a crowd.) That got Daddy so tickled that I thought he might fall out of his chair! Gaby and I still keep in touch via Facebook and still laugh about that.

# 14

## COMING OFF THE VENTILATOR

"THE SPIRIT OF GOD HAD MADE ME, AND THE BREATH OF
THE ALMIGHTY GIVES ME LIFE" (JOB 33:4).

Saturday's game plan was to spend the entire day on the trach collar. Keep in mind that while I was on the collar, I was off the ventilator, so my lungs were working independently. By the time Daddy left that day, I had spent ten-and-a-half hours on the collar. I had the speaking valve in during that time as well, so I was able to start talking again, too.

Sunday morning, October 17, 2021, brought a pleasant surprise. The respiratory therapist came in and rolled the vent out of my room after I had spent thirty-six days depending on it. While she was rolling it out, I cried. I keep a picture of the vent rolling out of my room on my phone.

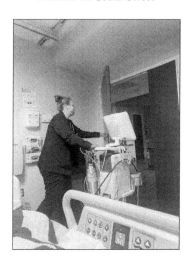

I spent almost twenty-four hours straight on the trach collar that day and was able to maintain my oxygen saturations on my own. My blood gases looked great. I was done with the ventilator.

While I was done with the ventilator, I wasn't entirely done with the trach tube in my neck. Since there was a dime-sized hole in my neck that went straight to my lungs, they couldn't simply pull the trach out and be done. This means we needed to gradually reduce the trach hole in my neck by reducing the size of the tube. There are different sized tracheotomies; the one I had was not the smallest available. I had a size six with a cuff. Ken came in and told me that he planned to skip the cuffless six, which is smaller than with a cuff, and to transition to a size four. This would allow the hole in my neck and esophagus to begin closing. He said they could possibly remove the trach on Tuesday. He also told me that I would have to stay two to three days after to ensure that everything was going as planned. That meant the possibility of being discharged without rehab and oxygen. He changed the oxygen in the collar to the lowest setting, and I was able to maintain one hundred percent oxygen saturation. I'm pretty sure I drove Ken crazy with my million questions, but he took one for the team and answered all of them the best he could!

Since I was on a feeding tube, I had not eaten actual food since September 11th. Also, after forty-seven days in bed, my muscle mass had almost completely deteriorated, and I'd lost fifty-one pounds since having the baby.

# 15

## NO REHAB

"HAVE I NOT COMMANDED YOU? BE STRONG AND OF GOOD
COURAGE; DO NOT BE AFRAID, NOR BE DISMAYED, FOR THE
LORD YOUR GOD IS WITH YOU WHEREVER YOU GO" (JOSHUA
1:9).

That Sunday was a really good day. It made me think that I might not need rehab and could possibly go straight home. A lot of my family wanted me to go to the rehab center, but I was very hard-headed and determined that if they said I could go straight home, then home was where I was going.

When respiratory therapy came in Monday morning, October 18th, they changed the trach to a size four and capped it. With the trach capped, I no longer needed the trach collar and could be transitioned to a regular nasal cannula for my oxygen. I had a tough time with physical therapy that day because I was trying to relearn how to breathe through my nose instead of the hole in my neck. I was down to only two liters of oxygen per minute. Latoya, the nurse manager for the cardiovascular ICU, came by to see me and told us that she did not believe that Landmark was the place for me. She told us that Landmark was more of a long-term rehab for those who are unable to wean off the ventilator at the hospital. In her opinion, home health was sufficient. We had some decisions to make, but that

59

statement did my heart a lot of good. I was determined to go straight home and skip rehab.

I had a swallow test to see what I was able to tolerate as far as swallowing food. I passed that and was able to eat some chicken broth for the first time in six weeks. It didn't taste good, but it was better than the feeding tube. Ken also moved me down to one liter of oxygen, and I was able to hold my own.

*She is one day closer to going home.*

When physical therapy came Tuesday morning, I was able to walk about 165 yards around the cardiovascular unit and maintain my oxygen. I believe they turned it up past one liter, but I held up well, either way. I also ate grits and some Jell-o for breakfast. This meal tasted much better than the chicken broth. My daddy knows me well and went to Cracker Barrel to get me some chicken and dumplings for lunch. It was *amazing,* and we have a video of that. That was the first actual meal I'd eaten in forty-eight days. I'd lost a couple more pounds for a total of fifty-three, but we were hopeful that the food would help me pack some of that back on. After my lunch, my feeding tube was removed! I was certainly glad to see that thing go.

During respiratory therapy rounds Wednesday morning, Ken walked my nurse, Gaby, through decannulating me, which means she pulled the tracheotomy tube out of my neck. The doctor gave me an estimated discharge date of Thursday or Friday. Physical therapy took me on another stroll around the ICU floor with less oxygen and was happy that I was able to recognize when I was getting tired and needed to rest.

# 16

# GOING HOME

"BUT YOU, BE STRONG AND DO NOT LET YOUR HANDS BE WEAK, FOR YOUR WORK SHALL BE REWARDED" (2 CHRONICLES 15:7).

*T*hursday was somewhat of a rest day, and they told me I would be going home Friday around lunch. They began swapping my medicines over so that I was on pills rather than an IV. We were able to change our tagline that day to "One more day until she is home!" Daddy let me type the update for that, and I cried as I changed the tagline. Many, many doctors, nurses, respiratory therapists, perfusionists, and physical therapists came by to see me before I left. We took pictures with a lot of them. It was bittersweet, Friday, October 22nd, as we packed my stuff and loaded it on the wheelchair to take me to the car.

Early in my hospital stay, my Aunt Kathy, Daddy's sister, said to him, "Bruce, don't you let the hair on her legs get long!" He bought an electric razor and shaved my legs from time to time, the last being the morning I came home.

When they wheeled me out of my room, and rounded the corner to a hallway, I burst into tears. The hall was lined with so many of my new family members. Doctors, nurses, therapists, hospital administration, and many people who had never even been a part of my care stood there cheering as I left. We took many pictures, and they had balloons, signs, pom poms, and so much love. Some of the nurses in charge of my care the majority of the time followed us to the car and helped us get loaded up. Paulette, one of my ICU nurses, made "Team Jessica" T-shirts for my core team and they wore them that day. They even had shirts for me and Daddy. Mine said, "I got it. I fought it. I conquered it. #COVID19survivor" I still wear that shirt.

Melanie, another one of the nurses, pushed my wheelchair up to the door of the car. While I stood up, they put my belongings in the car and opened my door. I walked from the wheelchair to the car to begin my journey home.

At 12:30 p.m., Daddy and I sent a text with a picture saying that we were headed home and had just pulled out of the hospital parking lot. Number Two was discharged and headed home.

On my way home, I thought of all I had learned over the last few days, weeks, and months. I couldn't count the number of nights that I'd lain in that hospital bed, terrified to go to sleep. While Daddy had been with me during the day, I'd had no problems with anxiety, but the moment he walked out the door, the anxiousness crept through my body.

My nursing staff on the CVICU floor at Memorial

Health University in Savannah did way more than I could have ever asked. They did a phenomenal job of helping me with my anxiety, but I needed my family with me. I missed my husband, kids, and Mama tremendously, but I sure was thankful that my daddy had been able to be there with me. Daddy has such a servant's heart and doesn't know how to say no to very many people, but one of my perfusionists and I will be the first to tell you that, had my daddy not been with me—and he was there every single day that he was allowed in that hospital, forty-four days in total—I would not be here telling this story right now. The anxiety alone would have killed me.

I will never forget the peace that God gave me throughout the journey. My papa has a friend who can pray about a person and then let their family know if that person is will be okay or not, through the answers God gives him. He will say, "God said to spend as much time with _____ as you can," or "They will be okay." When I first got COVID and was still at home, he told Papa that the baby and I would be okay. I learned later that he told Papa a second time, after the baby was born, that I would be okay. I had his words in the back of my mind during the early days of my fight with COVID, and I just had this peace that it would all be okay in the end.

Through everything I went through in the hospital, I never questioned why God allowed me to go through it. I just knew that it was a part of my story and that He was laying out a plan for my life. It was unclear at that time what the plan would be, but I was certain that life would not be the same as it had been pre-COVID, and boy, was I right.

My doctors, nurses, and other care team members also recognized that it was not them, but God, who saved me. This made a huge difference for me—it made it possible for me to see how God was working and how prayers on my behalf were being answered. The medical staff knew my life was a miracle from God; they were some of the first to tell us that. As I have said before, God had it all worked out. He had the right people where they needed to be, when they needed to be there. It was truly amazing to watch it all unfold, even though it was sometimes terrifying.

As Daddy and I drove through little ole' Screven, my cousin was standing on the side of the highway with her little boy, who had been on ECMO when he was first born and was scheduled to be decannulated from his trach during the summer of 2022. They had a sign welcoming me home, which was the sweetest thing.

When we turned onto our dirt road, I snapped a picture and sent it with the caption "I've been looking forward to seeing this sign for 52 days!" As we rounded the curve, I could see Mama, Fred, Chris and our boys standing outside waiting to see me. That was the best sight I've ever seen.

I did come home on oxygen, but I didn't have to use it unless I was moving around or just sat down. (My oxygen tended to desaturate once I sat down.) The climb up those five steps to my back door felt like twenty-five. Until then, I hadn't attempted steps, but I made it, and it was absolutely wonderful to sit on my couch, smell the familiar smells of home, and look around my house for the first time in fifty-two days.

My family let me rest for a little while and then told me to go outside and sit in a chair they had for me by the road. We were still cautious of people coming around me because my immune system was next to nothing after being in a sterile environment for almost eight weeks. Since so many wanted to lay eyes on me, my cousin Judy orchestrated a drive-by parade so that they could see me, and I could see them. I figured the parade out pretty quickly, but the moment my cousin Mike rounded the curve in his deputy's truck and turned his siren and lights on, the tears started flowing. Judy had even arranged for a journalist from the local newspaper to be there to document everything.

That evening, I received a message on Facebook from one of the respiratory therapists who had coded me. She felt led to reach out and tell me how God used me to restore her love of respiratory therapy. Her message said that after she got home the night I'd gone into cardiac arrest, she talked to her mom about what had happened. She told her mom that if I didn't make it, she was done with her career—that she would just find something else to do. So many of her patients had passed away from COVID, and it had taken its toll on her. Her mom prayed for me with her and told her that she had a feeling that I would make it. She said, "Meg, we are going to keep praying for Jess! She's going to be ok: I just feel it."

The first night home was stressful, as I was used to having nurses outside my room, monitoring me and my oxygen level twenty-four seven, so I set an alarm every two hours to check my oxygen saturation. You don't think about how comfortable it is having someone monitor you around the clock until you no longer have them there. To this day, I carry two pulse oximeters (the devices that measure your oxygen saturation) with me at all times. Not being able to breathe is the most terrifying feeling.

Saturday, my sister and niece came to see me, and we had a great visit. The rest of the day was spent resting and getting some vitamin D while sitting under the sun in the lounge chair after we did a grocery pickup—I got to ride around while staying away from people.

I sing on the Praise Team at church, and Sunday was a

tough day because I typically would have been at church. I knew I couldn't be there, but my heart wanted to be. Watching from home helped, though.

A few days after I came home, I went to Mama's house and sat in my usual chair. She looked up at me and said, "There was a time when I wasn't sure that I'd ever see you sit in that chair again."

The next couple of weeks, I stayed home between various doctors' appointments. Family members volunteered to stay with me during the day while Chris worked, and they rotated each week. The second weekend that I was home, I planned to stay home from church again, but Chris had to run the sound technology board, and the boys wanted to go. I didn't want to stay home by myself, so I loaded up and went with them. During the service, I hid in the corner of the choir loft so that I could stay away from people and give my immune system more time to recover.

After coming home, things between me and Chris seemed to be improving. We got along well, and didn't have many arguments during the first few weeks. I also required a lot of help doing routine tasks, such as bathing, washing my hair, and even fixing something to eat or drink.

# NO LUNG TRANSPLANT

"LET EVERYTHING THAT HAS BREATH PRAISE THE LORD.
PRAISE THE LORD!" (PSALMS 150:6).

*H*alloween was coming up, and we took Kameron and Kason trick-or-treating in our neighborhood. While staying with me one day that week, Daddy received a phone call from Emory University Hospital. They were following up on my lung transplant status and my place on the transplant list. I wiped tears away as I listened to Daddy tell the lady that she could remove me from the list. That was the best phone call! I'm unsure at what point the doctor told Daddy that I didn't need lung transplant surgery, but he had been in contact with my primary physician as well as my pulmonologist. Daddy was also the point of contact for Emory University Hospital, so they contacted him since I was no longer in a medical facility.

# BACK TO CHURCH AND HOSPITAL VISIT

"LET US ENTER HIS PRESENCE WITH THANKSGIVING; LET US
SHOUT TRIUMPHANTLY TO HIM IN SONG" (PSALMS 95:2).

*W*hile pregnant with Kaleb, I joined an online group of ladies who were due in the month of April 2007. I met several ladies in that group and have become close friends with a few. The one I talk to the most, Kristin, lives in Colorado. While I was in the hospital, she told my husband that when I returned home and went back to church, she would be there for my first service. Kristin flew in the Friday before Daddy gave the special service he had been planning since the week after I coded. I had known her for fifteen years and finally had the chance to meet and hug her. She spent the next four days with me, and we went to church on Sunday, November 7th. Outside of a select few, no one at church knew that I was coming. However, some of my medical team and out-of-town family came as well. I sang two songs that morning and didn't have to use oxygen the whole time. It was a day of pure worship and celebration.

Kristin's visit was short but sweet, and she left for home on Tuesday.

That week, I stopped using oxygen during the day, and it

was the last week I required someone to stay with me while Chris was at work. God just kept showing up!

*Most people who suffered conditions similar to mine never survived, but those who did usually required therapy and around-the-clock oxygen.*

On November 10th, four news stations from Savannah interviewed me with one of my cardiothoracic surgeons. I was also able to go back to the cardiovascular intensive care unit to see some of the people who took such amazing care of me. I hugged and cried with them, and we just enjoyed our time together. Of course, it was also fun watching the news stories on TV and the internet.

# 19

# FIRST HOLIDAYS

"BLESSED ARE THE MERCIFUL, FOR THEY WILL BE SHOWN
MERCY" (MATTHEW 5:7).

*B*y Thanksgiving, I had improved so much that I didn't need oxygen at night. Remember, I'd already stopped using it during the day. It was a glorious day when we parked the oxygen machine beside the piano, rather than bringing it with us every time I moved like we had the month before. I did keep portable oxygen tanks with us for a while, just to be on the safe side, but I never used one. I monitored my oxygen constantly, and if anyone coughed, I would monitor theirs too.

Christmas was extra special that year because we had come so close to not having any more together. We sat back and cherished each moment. Watching my kids as they opened gifts was emotional, knowing how close I'd come to not seeing that again.

Monday, December 27th, I had an appointment to follow up with one of my ICU doctors who was also a pulmonologist (lung doctor). I'd had a chest x-ray that morning, and when I saw Dr. Russia he was pleasantly surprised. He even called me Number Two! He showed me the x-ray, and it was *clear,* except for a very small amount of haziness at the bottom of my right lobe. He allowed me to take a picture of that x-ray as well as the one from the day I coded. My lungs weren't visible in that one because they had been so consumed with pneumonia. I asked what he thought about pulmonary therapy; Dr. Russia said that I could go if I wanted, but he felt it would be a waste of my time and money. What a miracle! I had been on the lung transplant list, and now I didn't even need pulmonary therapy. While I waited to have labs drawn, three of the perfusionists who took care of me came by to see me. I hugged each of them and we talked for about five minutes before they had to go back to work.

Shortly after my appointment, Mama went to the dentist. He asked how I was doing, and when she told him that my x-rays were clear, he smiled and said, "She got her new lungs, didn't she?" He knew God had been the one to clear my lungs and prevent me from needing the transplant. He was only one example of people's faith in God's ability to heal me.

The new year started, and things were slowly getting back to normal. It had been a little over a month since I'd used oxygen, and my oxygen saturations were back to normal for the majority of the time. Around the second week of January, my mama tested positive for COVID. She had a mild case, but we stayed away for the full ten days to make sure that I didn't get reinfected. Due to the severity of my case, the doctors advised against me getting the vaccine because they didn't want to cause a setback in my healing since some people got sick from the vaccine.

# 20

## COVID—ROUND TWO

"THE LORD IS NEAR THE BROKENHEARTED; HE SAVES THOSE
CRUSHED IN SPIRIT" (PSALMS 34:18).

On January 17, 2022, I woke up during the early morning hours and felt off. I couldn't explain it, but I did not feel right. Kason had a dentist appointment, so I took him to that and came straight home. As soon as I got home, I called and told Mama that I was not feeling well, and she told me to test for COVID to make sure that I didn't have it again. Well, guess what. I had contracted COVID for the second time in five months. I cried the entire day. I called one of the perfusionists and cried saying, "I have it again! I can't do this again!" He and one of the other perfusionists assured me this time would not be as bad because I wasn't pregnant and I could get medicine. They told me to monitor my oxygen very closely and if it dropped the slightest bit, to go back to Savannah and they would make sure that I was taken care of. My doctor didn't want to give me any medications, but he did. Probably because I was such an emotional mess.

On Thursday, January 20, 2022, I had another antibody infusion and I began feeling better by the weekend. I beat that awful beast twice!

Around the time of my second COVID diagnosis, my hair began to fall out. I'd heard that other COVID survivors also suffered hair loss, but I didn't expect the magnitude of hair loss I experienced. Like many women, following my pregnancies, I had lost hair, so being postpartum probably played a role in my hair loss at this time as well. Also, with Graves' disease and hyperthyroidism, hair can fall out, so I had a triple whammy when it came to losing mine.

Within a month, I'd lost almost all of my hair and decided that the best course of action was to cut the rest off. Chris and the boys were very compassionate while they shaved my head. Still, I cried the entire time. But, as soon as Chris was done, I looked in the mirror and busted out laughing. When I looked up, the only reflection I saw staring back at me was my brother, and I said, "I look like Justin!"

# 21

# SIX MONTHS OUT

"THE LORD IS MY STRENGTH AND MY SHIELD; MY HEART
TRUSTS IN HIM, AND I AM HELPED. THEREFORE MY HEART
GREATLY REJOICES, AND WITH MY SONG I WILL PRAISE HIM"
(PSALMS 28:7).

*A*round six months after my first battle with COVID, I had another contrast CT scan and bloodwork to confirm that the blood clot in my lungs was in fact gone. The CT showed *ground glass attenuation*, when the lung tissue is more dense than normal, resulting in a haziness on the CT or chest x-ray. This is very common in patients who have had COVID, and from what the doctors have seen in other patients, thus far, the attenuation may never go away. In my case, it hasn't caused any problems with my breathing or oxygenation. I followed up with Dr. Russia a few weeks later to make sure that the attenuation had not worsened since December and was good to go.

April rolled around, and Daddy had to have a heart catheterization. He'd had a heart attack several years previously and was beginning to have chest pains and pressure again. This happened to be the same day I had the appointment with Dr. Russia, so I was on my way to Memorial Health for that appointment. This was the same hospital where Daddy was having his procedure. When I was about ten minutes away, my step-sister, Karla, called, asking where

I was. I told her which road I was on and that I was close to the hospital. She told me that Daddy was having some severe chest pain during the catheterization and that Mrs. Karen (her mama) had called her crying. I put the pedal to the metal and whipped into the heart center parking lot.

I'd already called the nurse practitioner for infection control that I'd seen every day while I was a patient there to find out where Daddy would be. By the time I got to his room, she was walking down the hall, headed to check on him with the infection control doctor, Dr. Rojas.

When I stepped into the hall outside of Daddy's room, his nurse caught me. This man had not been a part of my care, but he knew who I was. He told me that he wanted me to know how much my survival had done to boost morale throughout the entire hospital. He said, "We needed that more than you will ever know." That showed that God had His hand in everything the whole time.

Daddy ended up being okay and his pain was air that had built up in his chest. After a couple hours, the pain subsided, and he was released to go home.

My youngest son, Kason, has struggled badly with separation anxiety after my illness. If I get sick or have to go to the doctor, he still wants to know if it's "bad like the last time." During my second COVID battle, he cried getting ready for school one morning. He wanted to stay home with me because he was not sure if I would be there when he returned. He also caught a cold shortly after that day and asked if I had been sick like he was. When I told him yes, he said, "But your sickness lasted a really long time."

His separation anxiety continues to be hard for me. I hate that my children have experienced so much and worry anytime one of us gets sick. When I have to go to Savannah, I usually don't tell Kason until I've returned home. "Savannah" has become a four-letter-word to Kason. He gets visibly upset anytime I go for an appointment or even to visit the ICU staff. He worries that I will be gone for a long time. Too long.

One day, I watched a show on television where a patient was placed on ECMO while in the emergency room. I watched in awe and was excited that I got to see what had been done to me and that I understood the terminology they used. That night, I posted on Facebook about watching the procedure on TV. Someone commented that stuff like that would probably bring back bad memories. But I don't have any bad memories from my ICU stay. I have a few that come from the time before being moved to ICU, but after that, I genuinely have no bad memories after that. There were most definitely scary moments, such as the profuse bleeding and the lung transplant conversations, but nothing was bad. Those medical professionals took absolutely wonderful care of me, physically, mentally, and emotionally.

In the months that followed my coming home from the hospital, I continued to make improvements and had gotten pretty close to normal, health-wise. I was able to come off all medications that I hadn't taken prior to being diagnosed with COVID-19, and I haven't had any significant issues. When I had the repeat CT scan to check for the blood clot in March 2022, they did find a small lump in my left breast, but it didn't cause my primary care doctor any concern. However, Dr. Mager, my gynecologist, wanted it checked out by a breast surgeon in Savannah. I saw the surgeon in mid-May, and he wanted to remove it to ensure that everything was fine. The results from my mammogram and what he could see from an ultrasound and biopsy that I had done did not match up. On May 24th, I had outpatient surgery to have the lump removed. It was a benign cyst that usually appears in postpartum women and goes away on its own. They just happened to find mine because I had the CT done for my blood clot.

Throughout my life, I had never wanted anything to do with the medical field, career-wise, but my COVID journey pricked my heart. I couldn't afford to go back to school to become a nurse, but I prayed that God would open a door for me in some capacity. I had developed a new-found respect for the men and women who choose to work in the medical field day in and day out.

# 22

## DIVORCE

"MY BRETHREN, COUNT IT ALL JOY WHEN YOU FALL INTO
VARIOUS TRIALS, KNOWING THAT THE TESTING OF YOUR
FAITH PRODUCES PATIENCE" (JAMES 1:2-3).

*Y*ou also hear of people who go through something as traumatic as I have and who then realize that life is short. With that realization comes some difficult decisions. I am not an exception to this.

Around Mother's Day 2022, it hit me that I was unhappy, and I knew some changes needed to happen. Due to the circumstances, I cannot say much about this situation, but there were some things said that weekend that made the proverbial light bulb come on for me. For many years, I had attributed how I felt to my being tired or stressed. It was that May that I realized it might not be just stress or tiredness. I was truly unhappy in life, and the more time that passed, the more obvious it was that I had some tough decisions ahead of me. My marriage was in shambles, and I knew that I needed to get out. I never told my family what was going on in my mind. Instead, I began praying that God would show me what to do for my well-being and the well-being of our boys. They deserved better than growing up in a home that was full of arguing and fussing all the time.

The last week of June, Chris and I had a vacation

planned with Kason. We struggled over what the plan for the vacation would look like with our marriage being what it was. Kaleb and Kameron had youth camp the same week, so they were not going on vacation with us. Eventually, we decided that Kason and I would go, and Chris and I would see what things looked like when we returned home.

Before we ever got back to Georgia, I knew what my decision was, and I asked for a divorce at the end of July. That decision did not come easily, and to this day, I still struggle with the fact that our marriage ended. It hasn't been a pretty process, but praise the Lord, my family has been a sound support system because I couldn't have made it this far alone.

Along with walking away from a sixteen-year marriage, I've also lost some friendships that I never thought I would lose. Still, Jesus has been right next to me through the entire journey. He has never left nor forsaken me, even on those days when I wasn't sure I'd make it through. COVID, or any traumatic event, will open your eyes to things you may not have been able to see before. It hasn't been an easy journey, to say the least, but I remind myself daily that God is right beside me.

God answered my prayers again during this time. I was offered a job in the education department at Wayne Memorial Hospital in Jesup, where I was initially admitted with COVID. In the past, I could have only wished for relationships like the ones with my boss and coworkers. They have supported me throughout the complicated divorce process and have been with me through a set of firsts following a traumatic medical experience.

# 23

# ONE YEAR OUT

"FEAR NOT, FOR I AM WITH YOU; BE NOT DISMAYED, FOR I
AM YOUR GOD. I WILL STRENGTHEN YOU, YES, I WILL HELP
YOU, I WILL UPHOLD YOU WITH MY RIGHTEOUS RIGHT
HAND" (ISAIAH 41:10).

This year of firsts has been an emotional process that I was not expecting. I pondered what life looked like as little as a year ago for two months. Some days, it brought a huge smile to my face to think about how far I'd come. However, some of those days hit like a ton of bricks and left me crying for days.

The first anniversary of the day I tested positive for COVID was very tough. Not wanting to upset the boys, I decided not to mention anything to them. Kaleb remembered, though. As I sat at my desk at work, trying to hold it together, I got a text from him that said, "Today was the day you and I tested positive for COVID," and the floodgates opened. I cried for the rest of the day.

Kason also figured out that it had been a year since I'd become sick, and he had difficulty processing everything. He didn't want to go to school, and he didn't want me to go to work. It took me a little while to figure out what was happening, but eventually, I recognized his anxiety. The administration at his school was excellent at helping me work through that time with him. The assistant principal would take him to her office to ease him into the morning and then check on him throughout the day.

When the anniversary of my cardiac arrest came around, I took the day off work and went back to Memorial Health to visit with some of the staff who had taken care of me. I visited with physical therapists, respiratory therapists, perfusionists, the cardiovascular surgeon and his physician's assistant, and several nurses. It was such a heartwarming day. The staff helped to lift my spirits, and I enjoyed my time with them. Reading through posts on Facebook also became a part of my healing process. It did my heart good to see how God had moved and touched so many lives during my time in the hospital.

The memories continued to bring joy until October 1st when the calendar reached the anniversary of my major bleeding issues. For some reason, that particular time period was tough to think about and re-live. It took a good two or three days to process, again, how bad the bleeding had been and how close I'd come to dying a second time, even after all I had been through with my lungs. I also felt somewhat isolated after my divorce, which made it more challenging. My family has been amazing, but my friends don't live near me, so in a sense, I have been alone.

One friend lives across the country and knows life has been hard for me. One day, as I struggled with the memories, the divorce, and the gravity of the loss that I've experienced, my phone dinged with a message. My friend shared the following with me:

"I would have pulled Joseph out. Out of that pit. Out of that prison. Out of that pain. I would have cheated nations out of the one God [who would] deliver them from famine.

"I would have pulled David out. Out of Saul's spear-throwing presence. Out of the caves he hid away in. Out of the pain of rejection. I would have cheated Israel out of a God-hearted King.

"I would have pulled Esther out. Out of being snatched from her only family. Out of being placed in a position she never asked for. Out of the path of a vicious, power-hungry foe. I would have cheated a people out of the woman God would use to save their very lives.

"I would have pulled Jesus off. Off of the cross. Off of the road that led to suffering and pain. Off of the path that would mean nakedness and beatings, nails and thorns. I would have cheated the entire world out of a Savior. Out of salvation. Out of an eternity filled with no more suffering and no more pain.

"And, oh friend, I want to pull you out. I want to change your path. I want to stop your pain. But right now, I know I would be wrong. I would be out of line. I would be cheating you and cheating the world out of so much good. Because God knows. He knows the good this pain will produce. He knows the beauty this hardship will grow. He's watching over you and keeping you even in the midst of this. He's promising you that you can trust Him. Even when it all feels like more than you can bear.

"So, instead of trying to pull you out, I'm lifting you up. I'm kneeling before the Father, and I'm asking Him to give you strength. To give you hope. I'm asking Him to protect you and to move you when the time is right. I'm asking Him to help you stay prayerful and discerning. I'm asking Him how I can best love you and be a help to you. I'm believing He's going to use your life in powerful and beautiful ways. Ways that will leave your heart grateful and humbly thankful for this road you've been on."

. . .

I hadn't cried that hard in a *very* long time. God knew exactly what I felt at that moment and sent His message through my friend. God is always on time, never late, never early. While crying from reading those words from the Lord, a song came on the radio by a favorite artist of mine, Jason Crabb. I searched my music app for more of his songs; the first song listed echoes my friend's sentiments. God hammered in His message. I may not understand why I have been through so much, but He has a plan, and He knows what He is doing. I just have to trust that His way is much higher than mine.

# NOTES FROM OTHERS

"LET YOUR LIGHT SO SHINE BEFORE MEN, THAT THEY MAY
SEE YOUR GOOD WORKS AND GLORIFY YOUR FATHER IN
HEAVEN" (MATTHEW 5:1).

*W*hile thinking about how I wanted this book laid out, I felt that some of my care team and Baby Eric's family may want to say something about how my COVID battle affected them. I asked several of them if they would be interested in having their thoughts included and several people sent me notes. I will introduce each one before including their words.

Hallee is a nurse in the CVICU (Cardiovascular Intensive Care Unit) at Memorial Health. She worked the night shift and was my nurse during those very critical nights I was on ECMO and the vent.

"Every time I see the ECMO machine, I feel a feeling of dread. This measure is a last-ditch effort to completely rest the lungs, heart, or both. When we put a patient on ECMO, it means we have tried everything we can to save them and this is basically our last shot. Because patients stay on ECMO for so long, the staff grows very close to the patients and their families during their hospital stays. Unfortunately, because of COVID-19, we had just seen a couple patients not survive after months of being on ECMO at the time of Jessica's admission.

"I began to notice that myself and other nurses started to lose hope in fighting this battle with COVID-19. No matter what we did or how hard we tried, patients suffering from COVID-19 on ECMO were not doing as great as we hoped. I remember after getting the report on Jessica's story, I went into her room to assess her and saw pictures of her boys. I told her, hoping that she could hear me—despite being paralyzed and sedated—that we were going to try everything we could to get her back home to her family. Tears welled in my eyes, thinking of these precious boys growing up without their mom. I said a quick prayer for her and her family, tried to push those negative thoughts out of my mind, and began my work. Little did I know, Jessica was a fighter.

"Over the next month or so, I watched Jessica beat every obstacle and grow stronger every single day. Some nights of her stay worried me that things were taking a turn for the worst and going to go downhill fast. But with quick intervention from physicians, perfusionists, and us nurses, combined with Jessica's determination, we were able to pull through. I also credit Jessica's survival to her unfaltering faith and her incredibly supportive family. Jessica's family brought in a cardboard cutout of prayer hands, which we still put in every single room that we feel needs extra prayers. Jessica and her family will always be very special to me and all of CVICU."

The next note is from another night shift nurse on the CVICU floor at Memorial Health. She was with me during those rough nights as well. She also helped with my hair during my hospital stay and would put my hair into a bun on the top of my head.

"Working as a nurse during a pandemic [that] was as detrimental as COVID was life-changing. I have been a nurse for five years and have spent the last three years in the CVICU at Memorial. The floor at Memorial has 32 beds. 10 beds are cardiac ICU beds, and the other 22 beds are cardiac step-down beds. When COVID was at its worst, we turned the entire floor into ICU beds because the Medical ICU was already full of COVID patients. We had so many extremely ill patients.

"I remember the night before Jessica cardiac arrested. I was charge nurse that night. We had 32 ICU patients, two of which were already on ECMO, most of these patients were intubated, proned (lying on their stomach) and on multiple drips. It was honestly complete chaos. We were all doing our best to just keep everyone alive and stable. As charge nurse that night, I had my own patient assignment and didn't know all the details of the other patients on the floor at the time. I remember Jessica's nurse came to me that night and told me that her patient (Jess) was requiring more oxygen through the night. I knew that Jessica was young, recently post-partum and post-COVID but that was the extent of what I knew. The nurse told me that Jessica wasn't oxygenating well on her nasal cannula and had a non-rebreather on over her cannula. It sounded like she was deteriorating but was otherwise 'stable.'

"The next night I came back on shift, I found out Jessica cardiac arrested. She was intubated, proned, and on multiple drips to keep her sedated and her blood pressure up. I heard the physicians talk about placing Jess on ECMO, and my heart immediately sunk. Although I didn't know Jessica at the time, I knew that if she was put on ECMO she would most likely never come off. Only two COVID patients survived ECMO: Jess being the second. Not long after the discussion of ECMO, Jessica was cannulated. I can't remember all the details of Jessica's course. I remember she was trached early on with the idea that we would eventually wake her up and walk her around, and I remember thinking to myself, 'this is never going to work.' I am typically an optimistic person and always want what's best for my patients, but we had dealt with so much loss and heartbreak during the pandemic that my hopes and expectations were at rock bottom.

"As Jessica's course progressed, she started showing signs of improvement. Once she got the trach, we started gradually weaning her sedation and waking her up. She got an Avalon cannula that was new to our facility. It was one big cannula placed in her neck that would eventually allow her to sit up and ambulate ideally. Again, when they talked about the Avalon I thought, 'this is never going to work.' But it did. Jess always defied the odds.

"I remember one time when Jessica was awake, but still a little confused, she was trying to FaceTime her son. It was around 2 am. Her nurse at the time, Kirsten, looked at me and asked, 'who is on the phone at this hour?' and we both saw Jess in her room on the phone, and we looked at each other and giggled. We were so proud of her progress but didn't want her family to worry [about] why Jessica kept calling in the middle of the night, so we ended up putting her phone away, and she was not happy. That's the night, I knew Jess was going to make it. She was strong willed, a fighter, and had made it so far.

"Jessica had her setbacks. There was a night I remember Jessica started having post-partum blood loss. She was on a heparin drip to keep her ECMO circuit from clotting off, but it was causing her to bleed. We found a blood clot in her bed that had to have been the size of a cantaloupe. We all panicked. She had come so far and was doing so well: we didn't want her to back-track. We ended up getting labor and delivery involved, and for a while, the physicians discussed the need for a hysterectomy but didn't know if she would survive the surgery while on ECMO. If I can remember correctly, we ended up trying to get her off ECMO faster because the bleeding was an issue.

"One night, we decided to wash Jessica's hair. Hallee brought in shampoo and conditioner from home. We did our best to wash it in the bed without moving her ECMO cannula. {Her hair} was matted with dried blood, but we did our best. I think there were four of us trying to comb all of it out at one time. I put it in two french braids at the end and hoped it made Jess feel a little better.

"Eventually, Jessica was weaned off ECMO. I remember the day she first walked down the hallway, and I know for a fact, most of the staff cried tears of joy. We finally had a success in the sweetest, most God-fearing patient.

"To this day, Jessica keeps in contact with all of us, and we all think and talk about her frequently. She truly is a miracle and a patient we will all never forget. She was our ray of hope during such a dark time for the healthcare world."

There are few from the hospital that I have kept up with a little more than others. Wendy is one of those few. She is a cardiovascular perfusionist who sat with me many times while I was on ECMO. She and I have kept in fairly close contact since I came home. She was so sweet to send me her feelings.

"COVID: a gut-punch to healthcare workers. Over-flowing intensive care units. Death all around. Over-whelming to hospital staff caring for patients and their families. Physically exhausting. Mentally draining. Feelings of hopelessness.

"Jessica came to us as a postpartum COVID patient who had suffered a recent respiratory arrest. The decision was made to place her on ECMO, the ultimate life-saving device. She spent 21 days on the life support that circulated/oxygenated her blood for her. She was in the care of multiple healthcare professionals 24/7 for a total of 43 days at Memorial. ECMO, while it saved her life, was not without risks. People who don't survive it, don't die because of ECMO, but due to complications of being on ECMO. Jessica had her own set of challenges being postpartum and prone to normal uterine bleeding, which was complicated by the anticoagulant that allowed her to be on the device. There were many days that the answers we were seeking as healthcare providers were not defined. It was trial and error, thinking outside of the box, and the continued faith, positivity and hopefulness of her father, Bruce, that kept us moving forward.

"Jessica's recovery was neither easy nor uneventful. It happened in baby steps on some days and huge strides on others. As a patient, she never ceased to amaze us. Some days were a struggle for her. Being awake and constantly coughing, trying to clear her lungs and expand her inhalation volumes was uncomfortable at times. But she persevered without complaint. Her father showed up every single day. He would encourage her, encourage us, and keep everyone abreast of her progress. Each day he would make a Facebook post about her recovery and end it with, 'one day closer to home." And then one day, he could no longer post that. What a blessing! Jessica was going home!

"After Jessica's COVID journey, she made a point to reach out to her care team and express her gratitude for all that we had done. But we, the team, had to express our gratitude right back to Jessica, for all that she had done. She was a shining star in a time where we felt defeated. She gave us hope when we had none. She proved to us that we could still make a difference, even when the future looked bleak and unpredictable. She gave us a reason to push forward and be the best that we could be. Thank you, Jessica for being the patient, friend, and now family, that we have needed during these tough times. You and your father showed us so much love, faith and healing during this journey. We are so thankful for the two of you! Hope has been restored."

Finally, Baby Eric's mama, wrote this on Facebook and gave me permission to share it in the book.

"Thank you all for your love for Eric! If I could, let me share the heart of our surrogate, Jessica—a true hero to Eric. Jessica contracted COVID in mid-August (the CDC did not approve the vaccine for pregnant women until August 11th). Eric was delivered via emergency cesarean at 34 weeks. Days after, Jessica was put on a ventilator, went into cardiac arrest, and died for five minutes, had blood clot scares, was placed on an ECMO machine, showed improvement, and then had uncontrolled bleeding due to delivery complications. For 44 days, we prayed for her life. Her family embraced Eric, Greg, and me through all of this. So many emotions for this beautiful soul who believed it was her calling to help another family become parents. The doctors said she had a ten percent chance of living. Her and her family's story of God's grace and mercy and the amazing team of doctors and nurses is a riveting testimony. We praise Him who carried all of us through this and are so grateful to Jessica and her family!"

. . .

This is the story of my tough battle with COVID and life after the destructive virus, but what I pray that you get from this book is the love and power of God. I know that every story does not have the happy ending that mine did. I was asked recently what I say to people who did all the right things, prayed the right prayers and still did not have a good outcome. My response to that very valid question was that God's answer to our prayer is not always the answer we want to hear. Sometimes, His answer is "no" or "not yet" which is very hard to accept. That is something that the devil has really dragged out in the forefront of my mind lately, and I have suffered from survivor's guilt. Although I never questioned why God let me go through such a horrible time with COVID, I have struggled with why God chose to save me and not others. I am working on it and have recognized where these thoughts and feelings come from and the guilt has improved.

I have heard that prayer changes things all my life, and I have now seen it first-hand. I had a conversation with Kameron a while back, and we discussed how he and my other two boys have seen God work in miraculous ways that many never get to witness. My prayer for you is that, through my story, you can see how prayer works and how faithful God is. The saying "God will never give you more than you can handle" could not be more wrong. He will absolutely give you more than you can handle, as you have seen here, but He will never give you more than He can walk you through. Cling to Christ in all that you do.

*"In this you rejoice, though now for a little while, if necessary, you have been grieved by various trials, so that the tested genuineness of your faith—more precious than gold that perishes though it is tested by fire—may be found to result in praise and glory and honor at the revelation of Jesus Christ" (1 Peter 1:6-7).*

Made in the USA
Columbia, SC
28 February 2023

12961294R00052